# TULLY AND THE CHASE

# Available in the Tales of Tully series

*Tully's Life*
This heart-warming story follows the journey of Tully from street dog to much-loved family pet, teaching young readers about the importance of kindness, understanding and hope.

*Tully Takes Off!*
Tully has arrived in her new home with her new grown-up, but she does not like it one bit! When Tully sees an opportunity to go back to her old life on the streets - the only life she has known up to now - she takes it with both paws. With a search underway, it is up to her new grown-up to work out what Tully needs and help get her safely home.

*Tully and the Sad Day*
Tully has woken up feeling grey and cloudy inside and she does not know what to do. She cannot help her big feeling because she does not know what it is. As her different feelings begin to work together in the wrong way, it is up to Tully's grown-up to help her to understand what she needs.

*Go To Sleep Tully!*
It is night time and Tully is tired, but she does not want to go to sleep. Her new grown-up knows that Tully is trying every trick she can to avoid going go to bed! With lots of adventures planned and Tully needing her rest, Tully's grown-up needs to find a way to help Tully learn to not be so worried about bedtime.

*Tully and the Midnight Feast*
Tully is a newly-adopted dog settling in with her new grown-up. Since her arrival, her snacks have started mysteriously disappearing from the cupboard and appearing under her bed, she seems to have forgotten her manners, and there are days when she just cannot stop eating! Tully and her grown-up need to work together to help Tully with her worries about food.

*Tully and the Scary Day*
Tully has woken up feeling scared. She isn't really sure why, but today feels like a very scary day, and she just wants to hide. Tully's grown-up is thankfully there to help Tully manage her big feelings and see that the day is not so scary after all.

*Don't Touch Tully!*
Tully is settling in with her new grown-up. She has learned that the new grown-up is a safe person and she enjoys strokes and cuddles with them. Then Tully starts to meet new people, who want to show her how loved she is. Unfortunately, Tully doesn't feel the same about people she does not know and trust. It is up to Tully's grown-up to find a way to help Tully with her big feelings and to be Tully's voice, when she can't use hers.

*Tully and the Tummy Ache*
Tully has a tummy ache and it's making her feel quite grumpy. She doesn't want to eat or drink, and she can't get comfortable. Her tummy is sore and it's getting worse! Tully is in a toilet muddle. So, Tully and her grown-up work together to sort the muddle out and help Tully to cure her tummy ache.

*Tully's Birthday*
It's Tully's birthday, and her grown-up has planned a special day for her, but Tully doesn't feel like celebrating. As the day begins to unfold, so do Tully's big feelings. Tully doesn't know what to do about the big feelings, so she does a bad thing. Luckily, Tully's grown-up is there to help her feel better about herself, and enjoy the rest of her birthday.

*Listen, Tully!*
Tully does not always like to listen, especially when her grown-up is trying to stop her having fun. Tully decides that instead of listening, she can be in charge. But when things start to go wrong, Tully and her grown-up need to work out how Tully can begin to find listening a little bit easier.

*Tully and the Makeover*
Tully has been having lots of fun playing in the mud, but now her grown-up says she has to have a bath. Oh dear! Tully is not sure she wants one of those. She is feeling a bit nervous about what is going to happen to her, but Tully's grown-up shows her that there is nothing to worry about. Having a bath is a good thing after all.

*Tully and Vera*
Tully has moved in with her new grown-up but she is missing her foster carer, Vera. Tully is struggling to understand why she had to leave, and whether it is okay to have big feelings about Vera. It is up to Tully's grown-up to try and help her to understand loss and endings and why, sometimes, they have to happen to make space for new beginnings.

*Tully and the Chase*
Tully loves to be chased. It gives her a feeling of excitement which starts off as being fun, but one day the excited feeling suddenly and very quickly becomes a feeling which is too big. Instead of feeling excited, Tully starts to feel scared. Tully and her grown-up need to work out how they can play Tully's exciting game without it becoming a bit too much for her, and causing a muddle.

*Tully at Christmas*
Things are starting to feel a bit different in Tully's house and all around outside. Tully's grown-up looks different, strange lights are appearing everywhere and people have started putting their gardens indoors! Tully is not sure what to make of this thing called Christmas – she just wants everything to stay the same. What can Tully's grown-up do to make Christmas-time a nicer time for both of them?

*Tully Goes on Holiday*
Tully has gone on a holiday with her grown-up. After a difficult start, things seem to be going well. But when the fairground opens up, with all its flashing lights, loud music and food smells, Tully's big feelings get the better of her, making her want to run. And she does! Tully's grown-up needs to find her in time to show her that holidays can be fun after all.

*Tully and the New Rules*
Tully likes lots of things about living in a house with her grown-up, but one thing she really doesn't like is all the rules! Tully thinks the rules are all very boring and her grown-up must want to stop her from having fun. One day Tully breaks her least favourite rule, and something bad happens. Tully doesn't know what to do! Can Tully's grown-up get to the bottom of this muddle so it doesn't happen again?

# Tully and the Chase

## TALES OF TULLY

## Jess van der Hoech

Trauma Tools
& Training

# Acknowledgements

As always, to my trusted editor Sarah Ogden for all that you do to make these books come to life. I will never fully know what goes on behind the scenes, but it is a joy to work alongside you on these projects. Thank you.

Thank you to my supervisor Linda Hoggan for your continued support, encouragement, discussion and much-welcomed feedback on this series. I learn so much from you and the knowledge I have gained form our conversations has been invaluable across my practice, the books and now this series. Thank you.

Thank you to Laura Benham, for your support in giving me feedback, the searching questions, your friendship and of course, the countless conversations about dogs, the content of which has become quite useful! Thank you.

A special thank you to Rachael Gartland for your advice, support and addition of a foreword for this book. You have an extraordinary knowledge of all things related to sensory processing and I'm so grateful for your generosity in sharing that knowledge with me. Thank you.

To the children and families who I meet in my therapy room, from whom I have learned more about hope and healing than any course could ever teach me. Your input, ideas, questions and answers are so valuable to me and I will be forever grateful. Thank you.

# Preface

The *Tales of Tully* series is based on the adoption of an ex street dog from Bosnia who came to live with me in September 2023. Watching her try to settle and adapt from everything she had previously known to fit in with a new way of life began to present a number of ideas as to how to communicate such difficulties that can be experienced, to others who are in the process of adopting or who have adopted children. The aim of the series is to provide an opportunity to explore different situations, circumstances, feelings and experiences, finding new ways of communicating and understanding each other, through the voice of Tully.

A short time after Tully first arrived in this country and came to live with me, she ran away while I was walking her and stayed missing for eleven days. For several months after that, I escorted Tully outside on a lead every time she went into the garden, such was my fear of her running off again! One day, very accidentally, Tully got outside by herself and rather than go and find a tiny gap in the hedge, she simply went to the toilet and came back in again. There was enough trust by now to finally let her go outside and know that she would come back in again.

After a couple of weeks of doing this, one day Tully started to play with me while we were in the garden. She bounced around wanting me to chase her. Every time I got close to her, she would dart off in the other direction, proving that if she was to take off again, I still wouldn't be able to catch her! It was a real moment for us because finally, she was interacting with me in a way that was purely for fun.

However, I noticed one day that after we had played for a while, as I approached her, she ran but there was something different about the energy of it. I moved my hand towards her when she was still, but she seemed to be frozen rather than just having stopped to rest and as my hand came towards her, she physically flinched and then ran again. I was mortified. I came to the conclusion that we had played the game for a bit too long, without connecting with each other again and so the trauma dance between the past and the present had begun.

This is something that I hear about in my therapy room a lot. The high energy physical games that escalate quickly, it being hard to 'bring the child back down.' When playing 'rough and tumble' or 'chase', everything is fine to begin with, and then seemingly without warning there is an explosion, with neither parent or child really knowing what just happened.

Being scared in a good way can be fun. We often seek those bursts of adrenaline; the quick 'highs' brought from riding rollercoasters, zip lines or participating in extreme sports. There's a reason why people enjoy those activities. They are predictable and safe; we know what to expect. There's a difference between engaging in an adrenaline-fuelled activity with a strong brain, and the same feeling being sought by a child who has experienced early trauma.

For this group of children, their world has not always been predictable or safe. There can be a quick switch between the enjoyment of a game and the adrenaline feeling good, to being genuinely fearful because the chemical has passed just beyond the limit that the child has the capacity to cope with. It is therefore important to ensure that there is regular connection between grown-up and child throughout the play, to help the child to stay grounded and in the moment, keeping those chemicals at a safe and steady level.

After I learned this with Tully, I ensured that every few minutes we pause for a few moments, she tolerates me touching her gently with a chin scratch and hearing my voice, we connect again and then the game can continue. This has made such a difference in her ability to learn how to play and for it to be enjoyable, stabilising her stress levels – and mine!

# Foreword

Having been an Occupational Therapist specialising in working with children for fourteen years, I have learnt so much from the children I have met. I have a particular interest in supporting children who have experienced early trauma and disruptions to their attachments; consequently they frequently present with sensory processing challenges. This has a significant impact on their ability to engage in daily activities such as school, hobbies and play with other children. Often these children do not feel safe even when they have transitioned to a new forever home, and they need additional support to enable them to begin feeling safe and grounded in their own bodies. This is because early traumatic memories are stored in our sensory systems. These sensory memories are imprinted in the autonomic systems of the brain. While the mind may not remember as the child grows up, the body remembers. Therefore when a sensory memory is triggered, it will activate their stress response of fighting, running away, freezing or shutting down. This mechanism is essential for our survival.

These ideas can be abstract and complex for young children to understand, and difficult to talk about in words. Also, talking directly about their experiences can feel frightening and overwhelming. This book skillfully addresses these complex and sensitive subjects through the experience of a dog, enabling children to think and relate to the issues raised in the story. We frequently relate situations to our in-house therapy dog to avoid direct discussions about a child's emotions and feelings. This can be a really helpful validation to the children.

Rachael Gartland

*Rachael Gartland is an Advanced Paediatric Occupational Therapist, Sensory integration Practitioner and Sensory Attachment Therapist. She initially qualified as an occupational therapist in 2010 at the University of Northampton. After working in Peterborough Child Development Centre for six and a half years, she set up her own company, Blossom Children's Occupational Therapy Ltd.*

*This is a therapy service based on the edge of Northamptonshire offering specialist services to children with additional SEN needs and to those who have experienced early trauma.*

*Services offered include Occupational Therapy, sensory integration, animal-assisted therapy (therapy dog), sensory attachment therapy and also speech and language therapy services. The small team work together with many other independent professionals to provide a holistic child-centred approach to achieving a fulfilled life.*

*For more information, and for more helpful resources, please visit their website:*

*https://childrensoccupationaltherapy.org.uk*

# How to use this book

First and foremost, ensure that both you and the child are well-regulated and comfortable when you begin to read Tully's story. Make sure you choose a time when you are unlikely to be interrupted. The child may like a soother, a favourite or fidget toy, a drink or something to suck or chew to help them to stay regulated.

If the child is calm, then begins to try and distract or move away from the reading, make a note of what they have just heard in the text. It is very likely that they will have just provided you with some valuable information about something that they cannot tolerate or want to avoid for now.

The questions have been designed not only to explore the internal world of the child, but to help to develop a common language between the child and adult who are using this book together. The child cannot get the answers to the questions incorrect. Their interpretation of the thoughts and feelings Tully is having may provide some very significant information about the child's own thoughts and feelings. The child may want to expand the answers to talk about themselves and may even be able to make comparisons between Tully's feelings and their own.

# Tully and the Chase

Tully was outside, sniffing around the grass. She liked being outside. When Tully was small, she had lived outside all of the time. She had been a 'street dog' and lived in Bosnia. Now she lives in a house in the UK with her new grown-up.

**How might Tully feel about being a street dog?**

How might Tully feel now that she lives in a house?

Tully had a garden that was just for her. No other dogs were allowed in unless they were invited by Tully's grown-up. Tully's house and garden were safe.

**What makes your house safe?**

Tully was busy sniffing underneath a hedge when her grown-up came out and called her. Tully was not expecting her grown-up to come outside and hearing the grown-up call her gave her a fright.

**How might Tully feel about her grown-up giving her a fright?**

**What might Tully's body have done when she had the fright?**

Being frightened had made Tully jump! She had felt scared for a second, and she felt this feeling in her body. When Tully had been a street dog in Bosnia, she had spent a lot of time feeling scared and her body had got used to the scared feelings. Even though she did not want to be a street dog again, sometimes Tully wanted to feel those scared feelings in her body again.

**Why might Tully want to feel the scared feelings in her body again?**

Tully ran towards her grown-up, letting them know she wanted to play chase. Tully's grown-up ran around the garden chasing her. Tully would stop until her grown-up got near and then would run off again as fast as she could.

## Why might Tully like this game?

Tully and her grown-up played chase for ages! Running and jumping and stopping and starting, Tully never let her grown-up catch her. She was really good at this game! They played it over and over again.

Suddenly, Tully stopped feeling the excited and scared feelings she had felt from the game and instead she started to feel scared and afraid. Tully's grown-up called her over, but Tully felt confused about what her grown-up was doing. Why was her grown-up chasing her like the big dogs used to do in Bosnia? Tully did not understand. She growled at her grown-up and went and hid behind the shed.

**Why might Tully be feeling confused?**

From her hiding place behind the shed, Tully could see her grown-up sitting on their garden bench. The grown-up was singing a special song that they always sang for Tully.

**Why might the grown-up be doing this?**

# How might Tully be feeling now?

Eventually, Tully's body began to feel calm again. She made her way out from behind the shed and sat with her grown-up.

"I think we did a little bit too much of the chasing game then, didn't we Tully?" the grown-up said. "I wonder if sometimes you like to feel the big feelings you get from being chased because it feels exciting and fun. But when too many of those feelings come, it can cause a muddle because you forget where you are and that you are safe now. It can remind you of when you got those feelings when you were little and sometimes had to run away because you were scared. That makes you feel confused about whether I'm safe or not."

## Is Tully's grown-up right?

What else might be happening in Tully's body?

# Is there anything else Tully might be thinking?

"When we play chase, we need to have lots of pauses during our game, so that your body can empty its big feeling tank so it does not overflow and cause a muddle."

## Is this a good plan?

The next time Tully and her grown-up played chase, after a few minutes, Tully and her grown-up paused and Tully got her favourite chest rub that helped her to feel calm. Tully remembered that she was in her garden, that no other dogs were allowed in without permission and that she was with her grown-up and was safe.

**Why is it important to do this?**

Tully and her grown-up loved their games together. By making sure that excited and calm feelings started working together, they were always able to have lots of fun. And Tully loved to have fun!

**What games do you like to play?**

What helps you to feel calm if your feelings start to get too big?

# About the author

Jess van der Hoech is a qualified therapist who has spent the last ten years studying and working with the impact of developmental trauma and, in particular, the assessment and treatment of children and adolescents with complex trauma and dissociation.

As well as supporting birth families, Jess works with looked-after and adopted children and families, using skills in attachment-focused therapy and therapeutic parenting techniques.

Jess is a supervisor, trainer and motivational speaker with a passion for writing therapeutic books that are accessible to children and families to help with the healing process and to increase awareness in the impact of trauma.

# Also by Jess van der Hoech

*What A Muddle (2016) ISBN 978 18381987 0 1 (Co-authored with Renée Potgieter Marks)*
An interactive, practical workbook designed to help children who have difficulties with emotional regulation to begin to understand what is happening in their bodies. A variety of activities throughout the book enable the child to start to explore these ideas through the story of Sam, while gently encouraging them to begin to verbalise their own experiences. Carrying out the physical exercises in the book can promote changes in emotional regulation. The text is written in a child-friendly, gender-neutral style, and is easy to understand for parents, carers and practitioners alike. For children aged 4-12.

*These Three Words (2018) ISBN 978 18381987 5 6*
Also available as an e-book. A unique therapeutic novel for teenagers with the aim of linking together the feelings, emotions and behaviours connected to anxiety, with some of the therapeutic tools that can be used in order to enable better self-regulation, increased confidence and different ways of thinking. The book is equally valuable to parents of teenagers with anxiety, giving them an insight and understanding into some of the issues that may be affecting their child, and potentially opening up a line of communication and a way forward between parent and teen.

*These Three Words: The Journal (2019) ISBN 978 18381987 2 5*
A thought-provoking and hands-on workbook, combining a series of practical exercises and tools designed to assist teenagers who are struggling with the symptoms of anxiety. Addressing the anxious responses in both brain and body, this journal provides the reader with the opportunity to discover therapeutic coping techniques and learn how to apply them to their own personal problem areas, before committing to a twenty-eight-day practice to promote good emotional regulation and reduced anxiety. The journal can be used alongside the therapeutic novel These Three Words, or as a standalone workbook, and it is suitable for use by the teenage reader on their own, with a parent, or in a group.

*Beastie, Baby and the Brand-New Mummy (2022) ISBN 978 18381987 3 2* and *Beastie, Baby and the Brand-New Daddy (2022) ISBN 978 18381987 4 9*
A therapeutic story that looks at the external signs of pathological dissociation in a child. Dolly's story helps children who have experienced early trauma to begin to understand, in a very simple way, what dissociation is and why it has happened in their internal world. Tools and techniques are included within the story that parents and caregivers can use to assist the child in the first stages of their healing process. Beautiful illustrations on every page enhance the story of Dolly, and help the reader to relate to the events that happen, to notice the methods Dolly has developed to manage her feelings, and to think about what is happening in their own internal world. For children aged 4-12

Printed in Great Britain
by Amazon